A Woman's Christmas

Victoria

A Woman's Christmas

Returning to the Gentle Joys of the Season

Text by Arlene Hamilton Stewart

HEARST BOOKS
New York

It is the policy of William Morrow and Company, Inc., and its imprints
and affiliates, recognizing the importance of preserving what has
been written, to print the books we publish of acid-free paper, and we
exert our best efforts to that end.

Library of Congress Cataloging-in-Publication Data
Victoria : a woman's Christmas
        p.   cm.
    ISBN 0-688-11663-9
    1. Christmas—United States.   I. Hearst Books (Firm)
    II. Victoria (New York, N. Y.)
GT4986.A1V63   1995
394.2'663'0973—dc20   95-7503
                                       CIP

11/95
MCL
18.45

394.2663
S

For Victoria ~
Nancy Lindemeyer, Editor-in-Chief
Bryan E. McCay, Art Director
John Mack Carter, President, Hearst Magazine Enterprises

Produced by Smallwood and Stewart, Inc., New York City
Edited by Laurie Orseck
Designed by Nina Ovryn
Text by Arlene Hamilton Stewart

NOTICE: Every effort has been made to locate the copyright owners of the
material used in this book. Please let us know if an error has been made, and
we will make any necessary changes in subsequent printings.

Printed in Singapore

First Edition
1 2 3 4 5 6 7 8 9 10

CONTENTS

Foreword

*E*ach year when I unpack the Christmas ornaments and carefully remove each piece of paper guarding a treasured memory, I think of my childhood, when the women in my family took command of the holidays.

Preparations began weeks, months before. My grandmother tended her fruitcakes in huge crocks, moistening them so that by Christmas they would reach perfection. And they always did. The scenes beneath the tree each year were more elaborate: a velvet Santa Claus, skaters on a mirrored pond ~ what magic.

Closets turned into safes as wrapped packages piled up. When I became the woman of the house, my holiday timetable very much followed the ones with which I had grown up. Traditions continued, and I added my own, like the angel and toy soldier ornament collections I began when my son was born and a daughter was dreamed of.

My Christmas has become very much like yours ~ holding dear traditions, keeping hearth and home in the spirit of a season of love and joy. In this volume such sentiments abound. I wish you the merriest of holidays as each year your Christmas memories become more beautiful.

NANCY LINDEMEYER
Editor-in-Chief, *Victoria* Magazine

Introduction

Christmas is the most emotional of holidays; it draws upon the deepest feelings a woman has toward her family, her friends, her home, her past. Much more than a commercial extravaganza, it is meant to be an intimate celebration, where love and caring are conveyed in the most personal of ways ~ acts of grace that go beyond mere showmanship.

But all too often, there is so much pressure to do the "right" thing ~ stage the big party, serve the richest feast ~ that it is easy to miss out on the real beauty of the holiday. This is especially true for women, who have traditionally been responsible for making the season's magic happen for friends and family.

A Woman's Christmas is a return to the simplicity and joy of this most wondrous of holidays. No overly elaborate organizer, no recipe book crammed with complicated menus, no advocate of late-night wrapping frenzies and season-long spending sprees, this volume instead offers ideas and inspirations for celebrating with uncomplicated pleasure. Above all, it demonstrates how the small personal touch is still the supreme gift of Christmas ~ decorating home and hearth with natural materials, selecting or making gifts of tender thoughtfulness, contributing time and energy to one's community, and enjoying the uniqueness of the season itself.

We hope these pages will guide you toward a lifetime of Christmas celebrations filled with the true pleasures of the season.

For where is any author in the world
Teaches such beauty as a woman's eye?

WILLIAM SHAKESPEARE

inter is a season filled with unexpected wonder and pleasure, a time of glorious contrast. Warm firesides after snowy walks, pots of forced bulbs tucked inside florists' frosty windows, remind us how vivid and alive this time is. It is a season of transformation, of extraordinary visual delights. In the same way that nature changes the ordinary into the glorious ~ overnight, pine trees are majestic with capes of snow, icicles dangle from real-life gingerbread houses, ponds turn into sparkling skating rinks ~ we add light and warmth and holiday magic to our world. As days darken early, and street lamps guide us home, the affinity for home deepens, especially for a woman. And what could be more in tune with a woman's generous nature than the time of winter holidays? Now more than ever, she looks for new ways to delight and comfort. Holiday greens, candles, ribbons, and gift wraps are gathered; gift lists scrolled; pantries readied with the freshest spices. Guest rooms sparkle; thoughtful comforts await the arrival of loved ones. And while all acts of generosity are divine, perhaps it

Elegance
from tiny effects:
Candles grace
a holiday tree, while
shimmering
brocade ribbons
conceal
the tree clips.

Beneath
a beguiling jumble
of holiday
trimmings, an
antique desk provides
ample space
for correspondence,
wrapping,
and planning.

is the small touch, the personal touch, that elevates the season's pleasures high above the realm of obligation ~ a sprig of holly tied to a guest's bedstead, a basket of warm muffins for new parents, a red rose boutonniere for a dapper uncle. It is the way presents are wrapped and delivered, the care put into their selection, the thought behind every kind gesture, that characterize a woman's holiday.

One of the loveliest aspects of this time of year is that it gives us the reason and the opportunity to surround ourselves with beautiful things: fragrant greens, exquisite gift wraps, opulent ribbons, charming ornaments, letters and cards expressing the spirit of the season. Creating a "holiday headquarters" ~ a place where you can gather materials, organize correspondence, or dream over a cup of tea in the late afternoon sun ~ will allow you to enjoy the happy clutter and chaos of Christmas preparation without feeling overwhelmed. It can be a desk, a table in a quiet corner, even a bookshelf or two. Make it your own with pots of flowering bulbs, seasonal greens, pleasing views or sights. Transform ordinary objects into festive ones ~ fill pretty pots with an assortment of pens and pencils in vivid holiday colors and glitters,

(continued on page 22)

Gentle, at home,

amid my friends I'll be

Like the high leaves

Upon the holly tree.

GODEY'S LADY'S BOOK, 1890

a demitasse cup with special-edition holiday stamps, baskets with scissors and spools and spools of tape. Use a spacious tray to keep everything at your fingertips. Make your desk chair comfortable with bright pillows and throws so you can review card and gift lists, update address books, mend a Christmas stocking, or just regroup after a busy day.

Of all the materials that go into the creation of holiday decorations, ribbon is perhaps the most sensual and glamorous. Airy organza, shimmering silk, gold-threaded brocade, luscious velvet ~ when it comes to appealing to a romantic's sensibility, ribbon is unsurpassed. It isn't just for presents, but for dressing up everyday things as well: bundles of fresh greens and herbs, stacks of guest towels, rows of gift bottles, even the simplest of outfits or hairstyles. Victorian women knew ribbon to be a shameless flatterer; in the hands of an inspired person, it can strike many different moods. It can be witty ~ the casual élan of an antique white silk blouse dressed with a Royal Stewart tartan bowtie ~ or peerlessly elegant, as when a dollop of delicate chiffon floats softly down the back of a beautiful bare neck. Playful or romantic, ribbon is the perfect holiday accessory for

(continued on page 26)

In an entryway, cranberry organza secures holly to an etched glass chandelier (opposite); roses and hemlock cascade from a bed canopy (above).

22

❧ • Creating an Ornament • ☙

ong before the age of dry cleaners, poman-
ders were used to scent drawers and help
preserve clothes and linens from pesky
insects. This lavender pomander is also a wonderful
ornament for a tree or mantel; weeks after Christmas
is over, its haunting scent will linger. To create your
own, you will need:

Lavender blooms (approximately 1 cup)
1 (3-inch) Styrofoam ball
Spray adhesive
A length of ribbon (12 inches or longer works best)
2 or 3 T-pins (available at sewing shops)

Pour the lavender blooms into a shallow tray or
plate. Coat the Styrofoam ball with spray adhesive,
then roll it in the lavender until it is evenly covered
with blooms. Tie the ribbon in a bow and attach it to
the ball with T-pins, or glue the bow directly to the
ball using a clear drying glue. Slip a wire tree hanger
through the top of the bow.

Set against
holiday greens,
slender
gold ribbon sparks
off a wide
organdy bow of vibrant
cranberry.

enlivening whatever it touches ~ a plain-jane hair-style becomes Kate Greenaway with a wide organza bow, a topknot goes from boring to soaring with a halo of satin petals.

Holiday greens are as compatible with ribbon as Christmas cookies are with milk, their natural good looks played up by the exuberant personality of ribbons. Encircled in peach organdy ribbon, the most modest bouquet of Scotch pine and heather is trans-formed into a jewel. A massive gathering of lavender becomes heartbreaking wrapped in a quiver of gold brocade. Bare paper boxes tied up with generous widths of checked ribbon and topped with spikes of dried flowers trumpet a country celebration.

To turn up the holiday glow, pair shimmer with shimmer. Set brilliant-colored ribbons against surfaces that can reflect their shine ~ gold-flecked organzas bouncing off the high French polish of fine wooden antiques, gold-edged tulle entwined in crystal, ribbon collars dressing up candles.

When it comes to ribbons and trims, the more the merrier. But gathering a generous supply means planning. Fortunately, there are many interesting ways to do this besides the conventional trip to the stationer. A search through vintage clothing stores, thrift shops, tag sales, flea markets, and church bazaars can result in many exciting discoveries. Small bits of trim, silk flowers, tassels, braid, lace decorations, and odd lengths of ribbons await the connoisseur's eye. Have no qualms about recycling pieces you have received tied on gifts; sometimes they are just too beautiful to throw away. If, in the course of a year, you save all your finds in a roomy basket or tin box, at holiday time you can give yourself the lovely reward of layers and layers of treasures. It is almost too good not to share . . . why not invite a friend over for a Gift-Wrap Tea? Together you may discover many wonderful ways to turn your collection into delights ~ an antique silk tassel for the top of a hatbox, a length of picot ribbon for a nosegay of velvet violets, stiff gold brocade perfect for wrapping around clay pots of amaryllis, a swatch of vintage black velvet pleated into a tight bow and sewn onto a barrette. And, what is even nicer, you can relate the stories of how you discovered your special pieces.

Decorating one's home at Christmas is one of the most generous ways of sharing. It is an act that transcends giving and receiving, existing solely to

A hard-to-wrap gift becomes mysterious swathed in amber tulle and accented with delicate lavender.

A
circle of rosemary
crisscrossed
with two spikes of
lavender and
tied with sheer
black netting becomes
a stunning
tree ornament.

create beauty for others to enjoy. At your front door, a bunch of holly, tied with bright red satin, is not only festive; an old English superstition assures that it will bring good fortune all year long. In addition to holly, all evergreens are prized during winter. Pine, fir, juniper, boxwood, and yew are bushy and vibrant year-round, suggesting the continuum of life and so perfectly suited to the Christmastime notions of birth and rejuvenation.

As beautiful as traditional greens are, there is so much more that nature has to offer us. Besides the hallowed holly, pine, and balsam, there is the wild beauty of vines, berries, pods, nuts, and pine bark. If we share Henry David Thoreau's observation that "Heaven is under our feet as well as above our heads," we can find a treasure trove right in our backyard. Rambling roses, now dry, can be brought home and given a second life with washes of delicate watercolors for bouquets and wreaths. All shapes grow bolder under a coating of gold paint ~ a wreath of amber-hued pinecones will shine like a beacon for years to come. Sheaves of overgrown herbs such as thyme, oregano, and rosemary can be twined in ropes across fireplaces and over kitchen windows; the

steamy heat of everyday cooking will release their intoxicating aromas throughout the house.

But there is perhaps no element more magical, more symbolic of Christmas, than the purity of light. The intimacy of firelit conversations and the candle-glow of midnight mass are just some of the scenes of high drama during this season. Candlelight, rich and extravagant in itself, should be used lavishly to heighten every mood, every object, every setting. Slender tapers, squat pillars, altar candles, lanterns, clip-ons with tiny cake candles ~ they all "burn so brightly/Beautifully lightly." Small candles whisper enchantment for two souls joined in a tête-à-tête. A grouping of flickering votives turns an ordinary late-afternoon visit into an exciting event. A tray of stocky candles encircled with lush greens and clustered in entryways warms and welcomes.

A feast for the eye as well as the palate, holiday foods become more delectable by candlelight, and even the most modest of meals deserves their brilliant company. To turn a quiet supper into a spectacular repast, mass beeswax candles in an assortment of antique holders. Entwine them with gold ribbons and ivy. Ring the necks of candlesticks

(continued on page 34)

Seasonal greens add grace to everything from family portraits embraced in a woodland vine (opposite) to a gleaming tableau of herbs and spruce (above).

31

Amber
candlelight bathes
a collection
of antique brass
candlesticks grouped on
a mantelpiece (left).
Gold cherubs
glow with bright halos
(above).

with sparkling glass bobeches. To set a gala mood, cluster scores of elegant tapers on the sideboard next to gleaming silver pieces.

The colors and scents of the holidays have left their stamp on candles as well. Intoxicating votive candles fill the air with their delicate perfumes; fruit-, spice-, and herb-scented tapers release the aromas of the season as they flicker far into the night.

At the heart of our visions of an old-fashioned Christmas stands the tree ~ stocky and bushy, with its hand-dipped candles. While today we deck our trees with electric lights, there is still a place in our hearts for the pairing of pine and candles ~ perhaps a balsam advent wreath studded with candles set out on the dining room table as a centerpiece, or suspended from the ceiling with trailing red velvet ribbons as a sort of natural chandelier.

Even though each year we invent the holidays anew, a woman's romantic sensibility naturally turns to memories of Christmases past. Over the years, the need for traditions only deepens, as they comfort and reassure us ~ the aroma of freshly baked cookies, the twinkle of beloved ornaments. We are meant to feel the joy of the season, not the pressure of overwhelming details.

(continued on page 38)

Simple holiday flowers and greens adorn family heirlooms and photographs (right) and a pair of vintage ice skates (above).

The circle of our Christmas associations and the lessons that they bring, expands! Let us welcome every one of them and summon them to take their place by the Christmas hearth.

CHARLES DICKENS

Often, it is the small gesture that infuses a holiday with magic ~ an impromptu serenade played at the piano by one sibling for another, or a special treat from the kitchen that you really love served in candlelight. The charms of earlier Christmases come back to us as their gentle customs are revived ~ making paper cornucopias for the tree, threading popcorn and cranberry garlands.

And each year, family treasures that speak of generations past are unwrapped and displayed in fresh holiday finery: leatherbound photo albums, scrapbooks, and dressing-table accessories. Great-Granddad timed the turkey with his gold watch; now it rests on the sideboard, bright with a red satin streamer. Family teacups are stacked on a table the way they would have been a century ago. At holiday time, your favorite collections deserve to be seen in all their glory as well ~ Victorian biscuit tins, beaded purses, crystal bottles, velvet jewelry boxes, pearl cameos, silver snuffboxes, whatever you love. Present them on gleaming surfaces throughout the house and they will mirror the happiness you brought to collecting them. They may be all the "decorating" your home really needs.

An antique calling card case makes a becoming tree ornament (opposite), as does a sparkling collection of pressed-metal stars and beads (above).

Back over the black mystery of old years, forward into the black mystery of years to come, shines ever more confident the golden kindliness of Christmas.

WINIFRED KIRKLAND

My Family's Christmas Traditions

_____

_____

_____

_____

_____

_____

_____

_____

_____

_____

_____

_____

_____

Heirloom Ornaments

Whispers in Santa's Ear

Whispers in Santa's Ear

estowing gifts on loved ones is a great delight anytime. Now it is especially fulfilling. More than just a season to shop madly, Christmas is a time when, by sharing, we gain so much more than we give. Generosity, whether a delectable something from the kitchen or the precious gift of time, is a tradition as old as the holiday itself. In making up a gift list, we also create a portrait of our lives, a mirror by which we can see how large we have made our world.

We are fortunate indeed if there are many people to remember, but there is no need to feel overwhelmed by it all. Gifts, to be conferred with grace, need only be well-considered, not expensive. Everything needn't come in a fancy box ~ some of the nicest gifts make their appearance in baking pans, flowerpots, and sewing baskets. "The excellence of the gift lies in its appropriateness rather than its value," observed Charles Dudley Warner. Thinking about what really pleases the people in your life may take you down different paths. Wouldn't it be lovely to add to a

With its holly red leather cover, this beautiful edition of Dickens' 1843 classic would make an extraordinary gift.

friend's antique clothing collection? Or treat your grandmother to a day's outing at a botanical garden? Perhaps it is a box of drawing pencils, a supply of personalized bookplates, the recipe for your lemon-ginger cake, a Peter Rabbit Wedgwood mug for a grownup who may require extra coddling. There are so many ways to personalize even the humblest of gifts. Monograms, once a drawing-room art reserved for young girls, are an elegant way to say "This is yours alone." For the linen lover, seek out vintage napkins, pillowcases, and tablecloths at flea markets, thrift stores, and church sales. If they are torn or tattered, cut them up to make a modern version of a Victorian "conceit" ~ a fanciful pincushion or a hatpin holder, for example. Delight a friend who possesses great confidence and style with an old top hat you have transformed with a filmy length of netting around the crown. For an elderly friend who enjoys needlework, a kit featuring her favorite flower and place ~ is it a Nantucket rose arbor? ~ would be certain to evoke happy memories with every stitch.

Finding all these gifts may also take you down different paths. All along Main Street, Christmas glows inside and out. We hurry along, making sure to

Looking as though Dickens himself might have browsed here, New York City's Three Lives & Co. bookstore is aglow with holiday warmth and cheer.

Beautiful
antiques delight as much
today as they
did a century ago:
Gold and black enamel
compacts sparkle
against holiday wrappings
(opposite).

pass our favorite shops. Confectioners sparkle with their Christmas editions of ribbon candies and chocolate fantasies. Perfumeries release their scents upon the air the moment we enter: bayberry, mint, and chamomile mingle with lavender and roses, all promising beauty and relaxation. Florists' shops bloom with groves of paperwhites, carnations, and amaryllis; their zinc buckets of balsam and ivy spill out onto the street. Inside the warm recesses of antiques shops, niches are heaped with books, needlepoint pillows, tasseled footstools, delicate lace dresser scarves, all beseeching us to carry them home.

The "best" gifts may not be in a shop at all. Few are more precious than heirlooms and keepsakes. A wedding invitation, once folded in the family Bible and now framed, would make a touching gift for a relative who is marrying. Santa always enjoyed cookies from a special plate; wouldn't it be nice to present it now to a family member who has just had her first child? Vintage buttons ~ jewels of silver, bone, jet, and mother-of-pearl ~ can be mounted and framed for a dressing room wall. Many early tree ornaments ~ fragile glass-blown confections or decorations handmade from cards, cotton, wool, and

(continued on page 54)

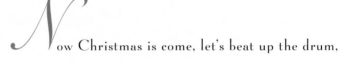

$\mathcal{N}$ow Christmas is come, let's beat up the drum,

And call all our neighbors together,

And when they appear,

Let us make them such cheer

As will keep out the wind and the weather.

WASHINGTON IRVING

tinsel ~ can be charmingly presented to the next generation when you hang them on their own miniature tree, the base resting in a clay pot and tied up with ribbon.

When doing Santa's errands, be sure to put your own name on his list. All too often, busy women see something they would love for themselves, but they resist because there is too much to be bought for everyone else. Humbug! Imagine how comforting a warm shawl or a pretty jar of bath salts would be after a busy day of gathering gifts.

Save a place on Santa's list for your home as well; a home that works so hard to please others deserves its own treat. A Victorian wicker breakfast tray will make life a little cozier on weekends. A floral hatbox holding rolled hand towels makes a lovely gift for the guest room. A nineteenth-century fruit-and-flower print dressed with a bough of evergreen and a playful plaid bow lights up any room.

And after doing all these errands for your family and friends, be sure to treat yourself to a quiet spell before plunging back into the mad rush of Christmas. Jane Austen, the supreme observer of gentle manners and morals, wrote: "To sit in

Fine satin ribbons are woven together to create charming little bags perfect for holding jewelry or lingerie.

idleness over a good fire in a well-proportioned room is a luxurious sensation." Give yourself this "luxurious sensation" as part of your holiday ritual. Stop at your favorite patisserie or tearoom, alone or with a special friend; you have earned a cozy corner, a bright fire, and the pleasures of quiet time and good company.

When your gift search continues, remember how soul-renewing a present from the earth can be. It is so easy to make it a botanical Christmas for someone you care about ~ greenhouses are bursting into bloom with potted hyacinths, lilies of the valley, muscari, irises. The bulbs themselves are pleasing. Place a small selection in a plain brown shopping bag, add clay pots and potting soil, then tie the handles together with sisal cord; slip on an oversize card, and you have made a gift that will last long after Christmas day is over. Or you might fashion topiaries of hydrangeas and ivy to flank the sides of French doors. A gift of a meadow of wildflower seeds will be appreciated by anyone with a country home. And a set of labeling sticks is as useful on a city windowsill as it is in a backyard garden.

There is always an extra measure of love in

A lovely young face from one family's past gazes out from a new brass frame. The border of ribbons is all the "wrapping" it needs.

An
assortment of
handmade
ornaments rests upon
a Victorian
crazy quilt, each a
glorious
Christmas gift
in itself.

anything handmade. Do you excel at woodworking? What about turning out blocks spelling "Peace on Earth" and a sleighful of painted Santas? Or are you a four-star pastry cook capable of creating bûches de Noël by the dozen? In this era of overbooked days and frantic schedules, a gift that takes time is especially cherished. But all presents need not be great time-consumers in order to be charming ~ tiny sachets of chamomile and lavender, bookmarks of brocade topped with a pretty pin, a personalized advent calendar, a stack of hand-sewn potholders ~ all are totally winning when topped with ribbon and a sprig of holly. A supply of chunky white candles becomes present-perfect in moments; just tie it up with cuttings of balsam or vines of ivy, attach a long stick of cinnamon, and encircle the grouping with gold ribbon. To strike just the right note for a hostess gift ~ it should not be so grand that it overshadows the hostess' own efforts ~ let the elegance of one perfect rose tied with a gold ribbon, or a tiny box of chocolate leaves, speak for itself.

An ordinary store-bought item can be made into something exciting, too. Spill out the contents of your nature basket ~ moss, pine, and acorns ~ and

(continued on page 62)

*O*n one branch there
hung little nets cut out of colored
paper, and each net was
filled with sugar plums, and among
other boughs gilded apples
and walnuts were suspended . . . little
blue and white tapers were
placed among the leaves.

CLEMENT C. MOORE

A gift
from one namesake
to another,
this amber-hued
silk boudoir pillow
is dressed for
holiday giving with
just a simple bow tied
with plaster
fruits and tassels.

A handmade
cardigan floats delicately
from a tapestry
hanger (opposite).
A bowl of knitting yarn
and needles might
make a handsome gift in
itself (above).

make a verdant fantasy mirror by gluing them onto a plain frame with a hot-glue gun. Scottish plaid was a favorite of Queen Victoria; steal a little royal thunder by covering ordinary boudoir pillows with bright tartan patterns, or cover them with swatches taken from old linens and tablecloths. You won't need a great deal of fabric; boudoir pillows tend to increase in charm as they decrease in size.

Every gift of food will receive a sincere welcome, for no matter how much a hostess prepares, there is always room for more ~ perhaps a bottle of homemade preserves, a box of bonbons ~ even Scrooge would have been delighted with a tiny tin of chocolate truffles. Often, the best food gifts are simple ones: a nostalgia-filled packet of three dozen candy canes for the tree; the extraordinary romance of a miniature sacher torte delivered with two dessert forks and frilly paper napkins; a pound of the absolutely freshest pistachio nuts packed in an airtight mason jar; a stoneware crock brimming with spicy gherkins or homemade corn relish; a dozen bagels for a city boy away from home. The simplest loaf of homemade bread becomes a rare treat when delivered piping hot with a stick of the sweetest,

(continued on page 66)

❧ ∙ Making a Gift Basket ∙ ❧

hether a pyramid of nuts and fruits, or a collection of beauty lotions and French-milled soaps, a gift basket should be as richly packed as a Christmas stocking crammed with treats. Roll half a dozen fluffy white towels in a wicker basket and tie a length of white satin ribbon through the handles. Fill a small Shaker thread box with chestnuts or a handwoven basket with holly. Make a fruit basket from a wooden fruit crate, picnic hamper, or fishing creel; a gilding of gold paint or a wash of watercolors covers faded spots, a weaving of ribbon conceals splits and tears. Assemble perfect, unblemished fruit, carefully washed and dried. Choose one type, or a mixed selection in one color family, such as green grapes with honeydew melons. Float in sheet after sheet of plain tissue paper (pink the edges for a textured look), then carefully add the fruit, putting the heaviest pieces on the bottom for balance. For long journeys, drape the basket in clear cellophane or tissue, then seal at the top with a sprig of holly or mistletoe.

freshest butter. Why not make someone's life easier by dropping off an assortment of holiday cookies a few days before Christmas? This would be so perfect for parents with little children and little time. Wrap the cookies in a pretty tin, then tie the tin up with ribbon and "serving instructions," and you are sure to become a lovely part of someone's Christmas Eve. A modest bottle of sparkling wine takes on a special mystique swathed in sheets of white tissue paper, then crisscrossed with a simple gold ribbon. Or a pretty tea towel can be tied around the bottle; long after the wine is gone, the "wrapping" can be pressed into service.

Holiday wrap can be so much more than the traditional printed paper with stiff bows and white cards. Witty, inventive solutions can be fashioned from the simplest materials: pieces of felt made into little pouches for antique jewels; crocheted doilies to hold crystal flacons. Present a loaf of brown bread in its own baking tin with a sprig of holly; jot down the recipe on the back of the gift card for a thoughtful touch. Small loaves of your homemade tea breads become big treats wrapped in clear cellophane and a swatch of wide taffeta. Start a child on a lifelong love

Jars of homemade sour cherries (above) and store-bought preserves (right) are wrapped in perky kerchiefs and caps of lace and linen.

affair with baking by writing down your favorite
recipes in little blank books; place the books on a
small tablecloth along with bags of chocolate chips, a
bottle of vanilla extract, and, most importantly, a
timer. Bring up the four ends and tie in the middle
like a hobo's sack. Thread potholders onto the ends
before the final knot.

Resourceful Victorian women and children
often made their own tree ornaments, such as paper
angels and lacy cornucopias. "Scraps" with images so
dear to the Victorians ~ children, robins, chicks, and
flowers ~ were glued to cardboard, then hung from
Christmas trees with strands of wool. Red papers
were saved to be cut into bells, and Santa's reindeer
sprang forth from twisted wire. Today we can borrow
many of these beautiful old ideas to wrap packages
and make gift cards. A paper punch, sharp scissors,
and glue are all that is necessary. Dip into your collection of scraps ~ even the tiniest snippet of lace or
ribbon will turn a gift card into a work of art. Cut a
supply of heavy card stock into 3-inch squares; punch
two holes in either end and thread the ribbon through.

Yards and yards of netting are a delightful way
to cover special presents. Bolts are inexpensive and

Taffeta,
grosgrain, and satin
ribbon will make
the magic happen for any
gift (opposite).
Velvet ribbons and
decorative berries transform
plain packages
into elegant ones (above).

are available in many different colors and widths, usually 96 inches and more. Swathe a gift in a cloud of netting, then close the top with a silk scrunchie graced with velvet flowers. Plain brown kraft paper and plaid ribbon conveys a country informality that is ideal for a food gift. A stenciling of gold stars, bells, or other holiday motifs on humble paper bags is sure to transform the ordinary into the sublime ~ decorate a copious supply before the holidays, then fill them with assortments of cookies to be presented to departing guests throughout Christmas week. Dress up a bottle of homemade vinegar in a paper lunch bag; tie it with a bow and add a gift tag.

For sheer romance, nothing surpasses shimmering French ribbon with its enclosed wire. It is so beautiful and costly that it is easy to see why it was used to tie royal documents sent between European capitals in centuries past. As lovely as it is as gift wrap, it would also make an extravagant present itself ~ an entire spool, wrapped in a swatch of silk brocade, a piece of antique lace, or a white damask napkin, then secured with the simplest gold lace.

Of course, not all gifts are tangible. Surely this is the time to turn an especially generous eye

(continued on page 75)

A hearty tartan fabric gets the feminine touch with a nosegay of roses and lavender (right). Plain boxes get new holiday life with a covering of grape leaves and a shiny gold bow (above).

Mon beau Sapin
Mon beau sa-pin, roi des fo-rêts, Que j'ai-me ta pa
ru-re! Quand par l'hi-ver bois et gué-rets Sont
dé-pouil-lés de leurs at-traits, Mon beau sa-pin,
Tu gar-des ta pa

"O Christmas Tree"

Traditional German

O Christmas tree, O Christmas tree,
How lovely are your branches!
In beauty green will always grow
Through summer sun and winter snow.
O Christmas tree, O Christmas tree,
How lovely are your branches!

O Christmas tree, O Christmas tree,
You are the tree most loved!
How often you give us delight
In brightly shining Christmas light!
O Christmas tree, O Christmas tree,
You are the tree most loved!

O Christmas tree, O Christmas tree,
Your beauty green will teach me
That hope and love will ever be
The way to joy and peace for me.
O Christmas tree, O Christmas tree,
Your beauty green will teach me!

A church
is cheerfully decorated
with evergreens
and pots of
red carnations (left).
A wreath of
balsam and pinecones
dresses a
lamppost (above).

ward. Sharing what we have with others is at the heart of this most joyous of seasons, and it is the community in which we live that should reap the benefits of the true Christmas spirit.

Caroling is a delightful tradition that originated centuries ago in England. Today, throughout villages and cities, carolers still take this candlelit walk during Christmas week. You can host a Carolers Party with something as simple as warm cider, a claret cordial, or mulled wine. For more substantial fare, trays of bite-size sandwiches, frosted cakes, and cookies are reviving and delicious. Before carolers go on their merry way, a small gift to thank them for their incomparable generosity can be waiting by the door ~ perhaps bags of warm chestnuts to chase away that chill in the night air, or sachets of herbs to simmer later on the stovetop.

Decorating one's home is another way to say "Merry Christmas" to everyone who passes by, to give something of beauty back to the community. A snowman on the front lawn reminds us of the playful gifts of winter. Hanging garlands of birdseed on an evergreen is a treat for our winged friends. Bringing a decorated tree to a friend is a thoughtful gesture.

Sharing its
gracious hospitality
with all who
pass by, this home is
ablaze with
holiday spirit, from
its wreathed
window to its candlelit
mantelpiece.

But it is the gift of time that speaks of true generosity, and is the most precious of all that we can give at any season of the year. Spend an afternoon writing out Christmas cards with someone unable to do her own correspondence; take along pens with pretty colored inks and holiday stamps to give them the flair you would your own. Afterward, take your friend for a drive by the shops to see the window displays.

Municipal libraries and museums need extra hands during the holidays to help wreathe doors and decorate trees. Neighborhood preservation groups often stage reenactments of historic holiday tableaux, which give so much to community life. These wonderful groups are often short-staffed; your expertise at organizing or sewing or acting will help their efforts. Volunteer to read Christmas classics to groups of children at school or the town library; bring along a pretty tin of cookies and you'll have their total attention. Leave a cassette of short stories with an elderly acquaintance so she can "read" at her leisure. Take a small group of children on a field trip to spot owls and deer, or organize a skating party with young ones to give their parents an afternoon of peace. The possibilities are endless when the heart is in the right place.

*O*f all the gifts I have each year

(Some sparkling bright and glowing)

I think the gifts I hold most dear,

Are the ones so green and growing.

<small>Anonymous</small>

The Best Christmas Ever

Wish List for Family & Friends

Songs My Mother Taught Me

Community Holiday Events

_____

_____

_____

_____

_____

_____

_____

_____

_____

_____

_____

_____

_____

or those who have mastered the art of hospitality, no time is more exciting than the winter holidays with their round of parties and get-togethers. The gifted hostess knows that hospitality is not merely decorating a home and preparing meals, but rather the ability to make guests feel welcome and at ease. All through December, homes are rich with opportunities to do just that ~ caroling parties, teas, tree trimmings, holiday dinners. No sooner do we put away the eggnog cups than out come the champagne flutes. But that doesn't mean getting buried in a flurry of fussy details. In order to entertain beautifully, one can entertain simply. A few eloquent details say more than all the gilded excess in the world, from a soothing frothy drink on a snowy day to a warm blanket at the foot of a guest's bed. There are so many lovely, simple things we can do that will satisfy the longing to please. A festive dinner party can be built around one dish, as could an intimate breakfast *à deux*. Sometimes the pleasure of a great meal comes from making it; guests will adore a country brunch where each has a turn to make fresh waffles; lofty bowls of

Joy

A petit-point sampler tucked with a sprig of heather and yew extends an old-fashioned welcome.

fruit (strawberries and raspberries are downright exotic in December and the frozen ones are quite good), jugs of maple syrup, and big pots of hot chocolate top off a gala that guests will not want to leave. On the other hand, sometimes the pleasure of a great meal comes from not making it at all ~ is there anything as romantic as champagne and caviar at midnight? Bank the bottle and tin in a huge silver bowl of shaved ice, then set out crackers or toast and two crystal wineglasses.

It is the imaginative sleight of hand that transforms the ordinary into the enchanting ~ the one perfectly poached pear swimming in a pool of rich chocolate, or a basket of steaming popovers slathered with homemade jam. Cranberries crystallized in ice cubes elevate a glass of seltzer into a sparkling garnet elixir; bracing hot tea served on a silver tray seems uncommonly delicious. An impromptu "picnic" after a tree-trimming can be created with blankets on the floor in front of a roaring fire, a bit of holiday music, and nothing more elaborate than sandwiches and soda. Even at very formal dinners, the small touch rather than the elaborate is the most charming ~ crystal goblets tied with red satin ribbons, miniature

(continued on page 91)

The sum is greater than the parts: Simple seasonal elements ~ holly, pinecone potpourri, Santa's portrait ~ combine to create an enchanting holiday tableau.

*A*nd all the loveliest things there be

Come simply, or so it seems to me.

EDNA ST. VINCENT MILLAY

a Happy New Year

felt stockings spilling with foil-wrapped chocolates beside every plate. "A guest never forgets a host who treats him kindly," observed Homer more than two thousand years ago. And today, it is still the act of kindness and thoughtfulness that reveals true hospitality, whether it is a basket of rich creams in the powder room to soothe wind-chapped hands, tea and muffins served by the fire to chase away the chill, or a basket of fruit ready for guests upon their arrival.

So often it is said that Christmas is for the young. But it is adults who create the excitement that children so enjoy. Just as we pass along traditions from generation to generation, could there be a sweeter gift than making Christmas as vivid for a child as someone once made it for you? Before young friends come to call, lay out bowls of Christmas crackers filled with trinkets waiting to pop open and paper hats and ornaments inscribed with each guest's initials. Tiny tussy-mussies of red carnations and a sprig of balsam enclosed in paper doilies may take only minutes to make, but think of the lasting impression on wonder-struck little girls.

You need not prepare mountains of food for children to get the message that something wonderful

Baked goods become special holiday treats (opposite): custard tartlets decorated with marzipan, a sultana tea loaf tied with ribbon, and a gingerbread snowman piped in chocolate.

is happening. Nothing warms up little hands faster than mugs of hot chocolate. To turn the delicious into the extraordinary, float a snowy mound of whipped cream on top of the chocolaty brew, then dust it with red and green crystals of sugar. Add a long stick of cinnamon as a stirrer and you have just minted a Christmas memory that will not soon be forgotten.

A century ago, families gathered in the kitchen to prepare Christmas cookies and fruitcakes. Today, busy parents appreciate an old-fashioned occasion such as a Gingerbread Party, where children can roll out dough and decorate their own cookies. Long a traditional ornament for Christmas trees, these sweet cookies are easy to make. And after their work is done, allow the children to savor their labor. Usher them to their own special table set with a pretty cloth, fresh greens and flowers, colorful mugs, and your finest silver. Photocopies of the cookie recipe, rolled and tied with a red satin ribbon, will make happy souvenirs of a delectable day.

Sometimes, it is not the food at all that etches such a deep impression but rather that thing called heart, made up of equal parts style and feeling. Before rushing off to buy the freshest foods of the

A

roaring fire and
fresh fruit
on a silver tray lend
elegance
to a quiet evening
at home.

Gold
laces and laurel
caress a
damask napkin (left).
A vintage
lace napkin held in
a silver ring
tops off a bonny place
setting (above).

season, take a few moments to ponder the meaning of the occasion. What is unusual about it? Discover that element and play to it. For a nostalgic family dinner, you might mount photographs of past Christmas celebrations on small cards and place them about the dining room table. Suppose you were entertaining a visitor who is far from home; serving a traditional Christmas dish from his country would be a thoughtful gesture. And certainly, if guests were bringing any pets, providing them with holiday bow ties could not be more appreciated ~ if the occasion was formal, of course.

But it is in serving that the true genius of hospitality lies. It is fine to do everything by the book ~ lining up all the forks in the proper place, keeping fingerbowls at the ready ~ but the real secret of entertaining is having fun, for ease and pleasure are contagious. A hostess who has let her sense of humor prevail by arranging a herd of gingerbread reindeer down the center of her table is sure to create a relaxed environment for her company. Whether you linger over after-dinner cordials at a formal meal or stand in the kitchen cracking oysters and jokes, put your individual stamp on everything you do. "When

(continued on page 100)

95

✒ · Chocolate Truffles · ✒

ith their intense flavor and sublime texture, nothing could be more elegant than chocolate truffles. A favorite of the French at Christmas, these bite-size morsels are surprisingly easy to make and require just a few fresh ingredients.

8 ounces semisweet or bittersweet chocolate
1 cup unsweetened cocoa powder
½ cup heavy cream
2 tablespoons sweet butter

Break the chocolate into small pieces and place them in a food processor with ½ cup of the cocoa powder. Pulse until completely blended. Combine the cream and butter in a small saucepan and stir until hot; be certain that it does not boil. Pour the hot mixture over the chocolate in the blender and process just until smooth. Cover and refrigerate until firm, 2 to 3 hours.

Scoop out the chocolate by the teaspoonful or with a melon baller, then shape each piece in your hands. Coat in the remaining ½ cup of cocoa. Refrigerate until serving time. Makes 18 truffles.

 Raspberry Sorbet

his luscious fruit sorbet is simplicity itself. While sorbet is traditionally presented as a finish to a meal or a palate cleanser between courses, this treat can be served on its own any time of day. Made with fresh or frozen berries, it is easy to prepare ahead of time. Serve it in long-stemmed glasses tied with ribbon for an elegant effect.

1 cup sugar
2 cups water
1½ cups raspberries
¼ cup raspberry liqueur (framboise)

Make a syrup by mixing the sugar and water in a small saucepan, then bring to a boil, stirring to dissolve the sugar. Pour into a container and refrigerate. When the syrup is completely cooled, combine it with the berries and the liqueur in a blender. Blend just until the berries are pureed, then press the puree through a sieve. Discard the pulp. Freeze the juice mixture in an ice cream machine for at least 4 hours before serving. Garnish with mint if desired. Makes 4 servings.

Looking just the way Grandmother would have served it, a simple tea featuring heart-shaped sugar cookies and fruit, warmed with candles and holiday greens, couldn't be cozier.

we see a natural style, we are astonished and delighted," said Pascal. Now is the time for you to astonish and delight. Instead of serving guests an enormous, intimidating beef Wellington, why not satisfy the cold-weather cravings for warm food with a meal built around a wonderful soup ~ a cioppino or potato leek, complemented with lots of crispy breads and focaccia (so easy to make). A relaxed buffet style allows guests to move freely, and if you serve your soup with a big basket of red-and-black checkered napkins wrapped with tiny cuttings of mistletoe, things should warm up fast! If you have invited friends for dessert, instead of buttering every madeleine pan in sight, it is perfectly fine to serve bakery goodies and store-bought cookies and breads. Pair them with cups of steaming cappuccino or espresso for a note of glamour.

In the same way that you do not have to spend a great deal of time fussing, you do not have to spend a fortune. Sharing what you have imaginatively is the real accomplishment here. Pluck ideas from the past and decorate only with the greens and flowers of the season, just as resourceful Edwardian women did. No need for pots of hothouse orchids ~ is anything more seasonal than the charm of evergreens? Small potted fir trees are elegant decorated or undecorated and with care will last the whole winter. Even the touch of evergreen says Christmas ~ a wreath encircling a punch bowl, or a topiary on a sideboard. Formal dinners or other important occasions can also be dressed up with the simple touch. Heavy sterling forks and knives look spectacular when tied together with burgundy satin and baby sprigs of soft Scotch pine. For a mood of high romance, place one perfect red rose and a red foil-wrapped chocolate heart on top of each snowy white napkin.

Occasionally you may be faced with unexpected company ~ a drop-in guest, or a friend encountered while shopping. This is no obstacle to the talented hostess; a charming tea can be created from the most basic ingredients. Serve delicate cucumber sandwiches (cut the crusts off white bread, butter lightly, add very thinly sliced cucumbers) alongside imported shortbread. Arrange them all on a pretty silver plate stand, tuck in snippets of holly, and your visitor will be made to feel like royalty.

If hosting a luncheon for colleagues, let them feel as welcome as old friends. All it takes to create a

A cordial moment: Raspberries enhance the nectar served in a crystal decanter and crystal glasses; gold ribbons and elm oblige with elegance.

warm holiday ambiance is a few small touches. As guests walk through the door, the scent of simmering herbs (so simple to prepare on the stove with powdered cinnamon, cloves, nutmeg, allspice, and water) immediately greets them. At the table, instead of a single elaborate centerpiece, arrange narcissus bulbs one to a pot, each tied with a guest's name in lovely script. Gather as many votive candleholders as possible and scatter them across a deep-colored tablecloth.

An afternoon making wreaths for a good cause can be charmingly capped off with big bowls of popcorn and warm cider. Even juice from the freezer can be warmed and laced with cinnamon and nutmeg to make an aromatic instant punch bowl. You need not have a mountain of fancy foods to make guests happy. Children in particular notice the way things are served more than what they are being served ~ tiny balls of ice cream, scooped into a large crystal bowl, then drizzled with a syrup and studded with candy canes, is infinitely more dazzling than individual servings. Even the ordinary ice cream bar can work magic: Unwrap each one, put a paper doily collar around the stick, tie it with ribbon, then stand each up in a champagne flute for a glamorous presentation.

A highland bower, complete with needlepoint pillows, crisp linens, and fresh roses (left), and a glass of milk and cookies (above) extend a warm welcome to houseguests.

*J*oy seems to me a step
beyond happiness ~ happiness
is a sort of atmosphere
you can live in sometimes when
you're lucky. Joy is a
light that fills you with hope
and faith and love.

ADELA ROGERS ST. JOHNS

Favorite Family Recipes

Favorite Family Recipes

Holiday Menus to Remember

Holiday Menus to Remember

ecause a woman brings so much to the Christmas holidays, this gracious time should treat her well in return. Robert Louis Stevenson called the changing seasons "God's bright and intricate device," and winter is one that encourages us to reflect upon the past and plan for the future. Though snow may blanket the ground, this is the ideal climate for growth and rejuvenation. The holidays are both a time to be in the world and retreat from it. Christmas makes a great many demands; busy hours are spent shopping, cooking, entertaining. But before this time flies away, it is important to break away from the bustle to savor the pleasures of the season itself. With the same love that you bring to nurturing others, nurture yourself, even in small ways. Put aside time for simple things that will refresh both body and spirit ~ a few hours next to the fire with a stack of good books, an evening spent writing to friends, a long soothing soak in an herbal scented bath. One hour sledding in the winter sun and cold will give you the rosy cheeks of a ten-year-old. Wrap yourself in your warmest velvet

Grace

To decorate your favorite refuge: A nosegay of carnations, lilies, and greens connected to a heart-shaped sachet hangs from a bedroom window.

A quiet afternoon sketching captures the delicate beauty of winter. Ceramic pots keep brushes and pencils neat, and a wicker basket holds papers and paints.

muffler, pick up a basket, and head into the sharp winter air. You may find holly, yew, boxwood, ivy, and pinecones worthy of an afternoon's sketch. Take a stroll through a botanical garden; the warm heavy air, scented with forced bulbs, may inspire you to pot up your own. For women who give so much, every day now should be like an advent calendar ~ opening the door to a new pleasure, a way to renew one's soul.

Holiday treasures and pleasures await indoors as well as out. In the days of crinolines and calling cards, young ladies were valued for their drawing-room skills. Mastery of embroidery and drawing was especially prized. These gentle activities are still welcome company on cold nights when the darkness descends early. Head for your favorite armchair or chaise, where you can spread out your embroidery or stitchery projects. Create a comfort-filled niche with soft pillows, luxurious afghans, and bowls of fresh greens and flowers, which release their scent in the warmth of candlelight. As the candles burn down, stitch a patchwork-quilt skirt for the tree, or make sachet covers from scraps of chintz and fill them with homemade potpourri ~ dried roses, lavender, cloves, or thyme. Or just cuddle up with your own thoughts.

Reading and
rereading the classics
can provide
much-needed relaxation
and private
time during holiday
bustle.

The noble art of wool-gathering always has a place during any period of heightened activity. A quiet reverie with a soothing cup of tea or an hour alone spent listening to music and indulging in a daydream will do wonders to refresh you.

For many, cooking is one of those solitary activities that provide a sense of creativity and satisfaction. And since Christmas often starts in the kitchen, where the aromas of nutmeg, cloves, and cinnamon hint of holidays past, this may be the way you choose to relax and collect your energy. For this most sentimental of all celebrations, Christmas foodstuffs are the delights of writers and poets and the preoccupation of the child within all of us. Holiday cookies, breads, and fruitcakes are vivid memories that return every year. A cold December evening can be luxuriously spent preparing family specialties. This may be the year to learn something new as well. Why not see if Mrs. Beeton was truly an expert homemaker as you prepare her steamed pudding in a fancy tinned-steel mold? Add to your kitchen library with gorgeous volumes, or buy yourself the good equipment you have always longed for ~ a fine cake-decorating kit, perhaps ~ then whip up beautifully frosted cakes that will devastate the diets of friends and family! If visions of chocolate masterpieces dance in your head, consider taking a course with a master chocolatier. If you are in the gift-making mood, tiny gingerbread replicas of your friends' homes make extraordinary gifts.

Other rewarding holiday activities can find a place in the kitchen as well. Here is where you can perfect the craft of wreath-making. The simplest ring of bay leaves is an elegant beginning; other culinary creations might include marjoram, thyme, sage, chili peppers, and, of course, rosemary, the traditional herb of remembrance.

"More than kisses, letters mingle souls, / For thus friends absent speak," wrote John Donne. Many women cherish the time-honored art of correspondence. For this charming expression of friendship, exquisite handmade papers and inks will delight the recipient as well as the writer. Could there be a better time to do this than now? Set yourself up at your desk, or take your writing box to the fireside, where you can pen long news-filled letters to friends far away or family members who can't be home for Christmas. Mailing holiday cards is still

The Victorians started the custom of the Christmas card with delicate holiday images such as these.

another tradition bequeathed to us by the ever-gracious Victorians. Begun more than 150 years ago in England, this social nicety started out as postcards printed with wishes for a happy holiday. This gentle way of greeting friends took hold in America; soon thereafter, the elaborate visions of happy holiday life we still hold dear appeared on cards and envelopes.

Because a sense of family is especially strong at Christmas, it is only natural that during this season of good cheer we have the urge to rekindle warm family ties. Why not spend an evening going through treasured family papers and photographs, selecting lovely bits of nostalgia to display in your home. Perhaps you are fortunate enough to possess recipes for favorite family foods that were written long ago by a well-loved relative; placed in gold frames and hung in the kitchen, they will create a warmth all their own. This is an ideal time for putting together family memories in fine albums or archive boxes. These boxes become wonderful treasure chests as the years pass and their contents grow in value. If you love the grace and beauty of calligraphy, combining handwritten notes with old photographs makes a lovely presentation, for yourself or as a present for

(continued on page 120)

A

tapestry-covered
album is as
beautiful as the
family memories it
holds (right).
Christmas cards,
lovingly collected, deck
their own
fir tree (above).

⤳ • Sewing a Sachet • ⤳

veryone loves gifts of fragrance, and among the loveliest are sachets, tiny bags of dried flowers or herbs to tuck in a lingerie drawer or closet. Delight a friend or yourself with the romantic fragrance of old-fashioned tea roses and lavender, or your favorite potpourri mixtures, such as rosemary, chamomile, and thyme.

For one small sachet, you will need:

> 1 (4-by-6-inch) piece of fabric such as
>   chintz, lace, or polished cotton
> 1 length of ribbon, 12 inches or longer
> 1 spool of matching thread
> .1 sewing needle
> ¼ cup dried petals or herbs

Place the fabric inside out, fold it in half, then pin the two sides together. With little stitches, sew a seam straight down the sides ½ inch in from the edge. Then fold down the top edge ½ inch and hem it all around. Turn the bag right side out and fill it three quarters full with the petals. Twist the neck of the bag and tie it with ribbon.

To grace
a pillow, dresser scarf,
or picture frame,
this heavenly creature
was first painted on
muslin, then
hand-embroidered
(opposite).

others. You may decide to add to your photograph collection, purchasing the beautiful frames you have always wanted or having new, high-quality replicas made of old, damaged photo images. There is a wealth of ways to preserve family lore ~ stories can be told with old cards, tickets, printed materials assembled in collages. Receipts for a cherished family heirloom such as a wedding ring or a strand of pearls, written in a beautiful script, can be matted on a piece of vintage lace and placed in an antique frame. But family memorabilia need not all be serious and elegant. Funny photographs you took as a child with your first camera or drawings of family members and pets, once just something you did as a lark, are now prized mementos of your own childhood. Put them in a little album to share with your family after Christmas dinner.

Knitting, quilting, embroidery, weaving ~ there are many hobbies in which the repetitive rhythm of our hands becomes a relaxing mantra, clearing our minds as we work and serving as an excellent antidote to the frantic preparation outside our door. Setting aside even just a few free hours for your hobbies ~ collections, for example ~ is another way to spend

(continued on page 124)

In those vernal seasons of the year,

when the air is calm and pleasant, it were

an injury and sullenness against

Nature not to go out and see her riches, and partake

in her rejoicing with heaven and earth.

JOHN MILTON

Outdoor
pleasures: relaxing in
a corner of
the front porch laden
with alpine-
inspired pillows
(opposite)
or decorating a rustic
birdhouse in
the backyard (above).

calming time alone. Domed snow globes, vintage tree ornaments, terra-cotta angels, garlands of Art Deco glass beads, antique Christmas cards, cookie cutters ~ hung from the tree or arranged on a mantel, they add great panache to your decorations. Your collection does not have to be holiday-oriented ~ any one of them will look wonderful displayed with bits of greenery or ribbons. What could be prettier than your prized baskets brought out and filled with fresh boughs of balsam?

As winter settles in, the need to connect with the earth still exists. Long walks will put you in touch with an outdoors nearly forgotten under snow and cold. And while we can't kneel in the garden and bring forth blossoms, we can find color and scent in winter flowering bulbs. High-quality narcissus and amaryllis are the salvation of the snowbound gardener, their vivid beauty so reliable and glamorous. Pots of them mixed with boughs of evergreens are heavenly arranged on mantels or framing doorways. Garden catalogs arrive weekly now, begging for attention, just when there is little time to study them. Wouldn't it be lovely to make the time to plan just one special thing ~ a secret rose garden, a patch

of herbs for potpourri, or an urn of holly and ivy to commemorate the promise of winter.

"In December, keep yourself warm and sleep" was the adage of monks long ago. For when winter behaves badly, what could be more pleasant than a nap, an afternoon of sweet repose? So well deserved now, your sleep should be made as comfortable as possible, whether a catnap in front of the fire or a serious beauty sleep with eye masks and lotions. Laces and linens, needlepoint pillows, good reading lights, small boxes of candy, fragrant sachets ~ you are entitled to it all as you unwind, as you let go of the demands of the day. A long warm soak in a scent-filled bath will have you glowing, ready to nod off.

Curl up on a divan wrapped in a luxurious cashmere shawl. Or set an overstuffed footstool by the fire, feet up from the labors of the day, a cup of mulled wine in arm's reach. Wherever your refuge is, surround yourself with a generous supply of plump pillows, warm throws, and your favorite books. Draw the curtains, take the phone off the hook, and let the balm of sleep massage away your cares.

If the approaching evening includes a holiday party, indulge yourself by wearing your prettiest

(continued on page 130)

Wool challis throws, fine books, and candlelight complete a quiet refuge (left). The needlepoint sampler guarantees peace (above).

⤞ • Holiday Herbal Bath • ⤝

ne of the secrets of wise women longing for a moment of calmness at holiday time is the luxurious bath ~ not a quick scrub and shampoo, but a languorous experience that pampers you from head to toe. As the season grows more hectic, indulge yourself. Gather bath supplies in beautiful bottles, and surround yourself with luxuries simple or sophisticated ~ imported soaps, natural sponges to stimulate the skin, crystal atomizers of your favorite scents. Bring in stacks of fluffy towels, sweet flowers, a cassette of soothing music.

To create an herbal bath for a cold winter's day, combine sprigs of rosemary with dried rosebuds, bay leaves, and crushed cinnamon in a bowl. Pour in a cupful of lukewarm water and allow it to steep, even if only briefly. To this mixture, add 3 or 4 drops each of rosemary oil and rose oil. Sprinkle this over your bathwater, and allow the fragrance to pervade the room before sinking in for a peaceful interlude.

clothes and jewelry. If there is any season that speaks to the glamorous sophisticate in all of us, it is Christmastime, when engagement books fill up with occasions that encourage a high degree of finery. Whether stepping out for a gala performance of *The Nutcracker Suite* or sitting down to a candlelit dinner at home for two, take the time to give yourself extra attention. Start your holiday mood early with special touches in your boudoir. Tie back the curtains with ribbons and small bunches of holly or sweet-smelling pine. Perfume the air with your favorite scented candles. A demitasse of cappuccino or a glass of champagne will warm you while you decide what to wear. And remember to prepare a welcome for your return ~ attach a delicately perfumed sachet to your favorite robe so that it can weave a web of scent while you are away.

Let your dressing table overflow with the elegance of crystal bottles of favorite perfumes, lotions, and powders. Weave a pretty ribbon through your hair, and try out new makeup for a radiant holiday face. Crown your new look with more romance ~ hair clips of ribbons and pearls and ropes of golden braid to hold curls in upswept elegance. One simple

A collection of antique cranberry glass gleams next to polished silver (opposite). Rare crystal flacons sparkle in a dressing table mirror (above).

The
romance of the
season is captured in a
long cloak of
holly-red wool, trimmed
in faux fur (left).
A deep garnet necklace
glows beside
a matching cut-crystal
scent bottle (above).

flower ~ perhaps a camellia or gardenia ~ worn at the nape of a bare neck could not be more beautiful. Under the spell of a winter's night, the artist in all of us can be released with just the smallest gesture. Nothing is too dramatic now: wools of hunter green and burgundy, a magnificent tartan skirt topped with a close-cropped vintage velvet jacket and high-necked silk blouse, velvet cloaks of midnight blue fastened with antique clasps of sparkling gemstones, an embroidered satin waistcoat paired with layers and layers of linen petticoats. Beaded handbags, antique gold calling card cases, or evening purses of satin dangle from arms dressed in the most sensual kid leathers and supple suedes. Reminiscent of Victorian fashions, satiny ballerina slippers and high-top boots glide across dance floors. For a more informal eggnog party at home, a cashmere sweater goes perfectly with a pearl necklace and a long skirt; a simple satin ribbon in lustrous hair is a lovely finishing touch.

Surround yourself with the heirlooms your mother and grandmother wore: brooches of jet, coral, and agate with intricate gold settings, pearl earrings, initialed lockets and rings. For a sparkle

At home
in holiday style: Step into
an antique cotton
Victorian dressing gown
crowned with its
own nosegay (opposite),
or sink into a
luxurious pile of handmade
pillows (above).

of the past, hang a gold watch fob across the front of a tight-waisted black riding jacket. A lace handkerchief peeking out of a pocket is a bright exclamation point.

If an entire evening cocooned inside appeals to you ~ writing cards, embroidering, reading ~ relax in comfort enveloped in the embrace of your best robes and nightclothes. Blustery nights call for toasty layers; the lightest Union suit or long silk underwear topped with old-fashioned nightshirts and dressing gowns will make you feel as romantic as you look. Include extra comforts in your nighttime ritual. Adorn snack trays with holiday greens, and use your finest china and silverware.

Return to the pleasures of simpler times ~ make popcorn in the fireplace with a long-handled popper, play the piano to your heart's content, cuddle up in bed with that great English comfort, a hot water bottle wrapped in its own woolen cozy. If late-night revels keep you from home, prepare for your return as you would for a guest's. Lay out a luxurious night-gown and stacks of fluffy towels, turn down the covers, plump up the pillows, and draw the curtains. Dream of tomorrow. It will be Christmas.

*W*e shall find peace.

We shall hear the angels.

We shall see the sky sparkling

with diamonds.

ANTON CHEKHOV

❧ My Christmas Card List ❧

❦ My Christmas Card List ❦

_____

_____

_____

_____

_____

_____

_____

_____

_____

_____

_____

_____

❧ A Dream Day to Myself ❧

_____

_____

_____

_____

_____

_____

_____

_____

_____

_____

_____

_____